NATIONAL
GEOGRAPHIC
KiDS

LITTLE KIDS
FIRST
Nature
Guide

BIRDS

Moira Rose Donohue

NATIONAL GEOGRAPHIC
WASHINGTON, D.C.

Table of CONTENTS

GAMBEL'S
QUAIL

EUROPEAN GOLDFINCH

SANDHILL CRANES

GILA WOODPECKER

CANADA GOOSE

AMERICAN FLAMINGO

Wide World of Birds

RUBY-THROATED HUMMINGBIRD

Birds live all over the world. They live in forests, fields, deserts, and cities. Some float and dive in lakes and oceans. Some birds fly high in the sky, and other birds never leave the ground.

No matter where you live, you can probably see—and hear—birds!

IN WINTER, SOME BIRDS THAT LIVE IN COLD PLACES MOVE TO WARMER PLACES TO FIND FOOD. **THIS IS CALLED MIGRATING.**

SANDHILL CRANES

LAKES & RIVERS:
MALLARD

ANTARCTICA:
EMPEROR
PENGUIN

LOWLANDS
& DESERTS:
ROADRUNNER

FORESTS:
RED-BELLIED
WOODPECKER

CITIES:
PIGEON

OPEN FIELDS:
RED-TAILED
HAWK

Let's Bird-Watch!

To find birds, use your senses. Use your eyes to look up and all around. Don't forget to look on the ground for clues like cracked seeds and bird poop. Use your ears to listen for tweets and cheeps.

Shhhh! When you find an interesting bird, stay very quiet and still. Pay attention to its shape, size, and color. Watch how the bird acts, and listen to the sounds it makes. This is how bird-watchers identify birds.

EURASIAN SCOPS-OWL

If you find a **word you don't know,** look it up in the **glossary on page 46.**

STAY SAFE!

Be kind and careful around birds. Don't chase birds—it scares them. Bird feeders can be a great way to attract birds to your yard. But never feed birds human food—even if they really seem to want it. It's not good for them.

HOUSE FINCH

WHAT TO BRING

AN ORNITHOLOGIST IS A SCIENTIST WHO **STUDIES BIRDS.**

1. A notebook and a pencil to write down or draw what you see.

2. Binoculars to help you see up close.

3. Your curiosity, a grown-up to help you explore—**and this book!**

Feathered Friends

Birds are animals, and so are you. Like humans, birds have a backbone inside their bodies and they breathe air. But one thing makes them different from all other animals today: Birds have feathers!

There are **more than 10,000 kinds of birds** in the world.

BARN SWALLOWS

SCARLET TANAGER

EMPEROR PENGUIN

BALD EAGLE

ANHINGA

AMERICAN KESTREL

BODY PARTS OF A BIRD

When you spot a bird, see if you can identify some of these body parts.

HEAD

BEAK

THROAT

BACK

BEAKS ARE ALSO CALLED **BILLS.** BIRDS USE THEM TO EAT.

CHEST

BELLY

LEG

FOOT

WING

FEATHERS HELP BIRDS STAY WARM, KEEP DRY, AND FLY!

BLUE JAY

TAIL

Eggs and Chicks

Mother birds lay their eggs in nests, in trees and shrubs, on the ground, and even on rooftops! They sit on their eggs to keep them warm until they hatch.

Many birds, like this American robin, are helpless when they hatch from their eggs. They need their parents to feed and take care of them. Here's how they grow up:

1 EGG. The baby bird breaks open the shell with its beak.

2 HATCHLING. The brand-new baby bird is called a hatchling. It does not have many feathers. It is hungry! Its parents bring it food.

3 FLEDGLING. The young bird grows feathers. It can leave the nest for a short time to hop about, but it still needs help from its parents.

4 ADULT. About four weeks after hatching, the bird has all its feathers. Now it can fly and live on its own.

Some birds, like this wood duck, can do things for themselves soon after they hatch.

1 EGG. When this chick cracks open its egg, it already has soft feathers called down.

2 DUCKLING. Within a day, the duckling can jump, walk, swim, and find its own food.

3 ADULT. The duck grows a new set of feathers and learns to fly. Now it is grown up and can leave its mother.

Turn the page to **meet some remarkable birds!**

Fluttering Hummingbirds

These tiny birds move their wings so fast you can't see them flapping—but you can hear them! Their wings make a humming sound.

ANNA'S HUMMINGBIRD

MY SIZE: about as long as a playing card

MY HOME: open forests and backyards on the Pacific coast of North America

MY FOOD: flower nectar and tiny bugs

MY SOUND: *chit, chit, chid-it, chit*

HUMMINGBIRDS CAN FLY FORWARD, BACKWARD, AND EVEN **UPSIDE DOWN.**

Hummingbirds can hover in one place, like a helicopter. This helps them feed on the sweet juice in flowers.

LESSER VIOLETEAR

A HUMMINGBIRD CAN VISIT **1,000 TO 2,000 FLOWERS A DAY** TO DRINK NECTAR.

MEET MORE HUMMINGBIRDS

BEE HUMMINGBIRD
This super tiny hummingbird weighs less than a dime.

MARVELOUS SPATULETAIL
The male spatuletail waves around its long feathers to show off to females.

GIANT HUMMINGBIRD
This hummingbird is about as long as a banana.

Peck, Woodpeckers!

Rat-a-tat-tat! That's the sound of a woodpecker pecking at a tree with its beak. It's looking for yummy ants or other insects living under the tree bark. If it finds some, it scoops them out with its spiny, sticky tongue.

CHECK ME OUT! PILEATED WOODPECKER

MY SIZE: about the size of a bowling pin

MY HOME: forests in North America

MY FOOD: insects, fruits, and nuts

MY SOUND: *kee-kee-kee*

WHICH
WOODPECKER
DO YOU
LIKE?

ACORN WOODPECKER

This bird eats acorns. It stores them in holes that it drills in trees.

YELLOW-BELLIED SAPSUCKER

This woodpecker slurps sap from holes it pecks in tree bark.

EURASIAN WRYNECK

To scare off predators, this woodpecker twists its neck so it looks like a snake.

Crested Cardinals

Male and female northern cardinals look different. Females are brown with reddish wings. Males are bright red. Both have a special group of feathers on top of their heads, called a crest.

WHEN CARDINALS ARE EXCITED OR UPSET, **THEIR CRESTS STICK UP.**

CHECK ME OUT! NORTHERN CARDINAL

MY SIZE: about as long as a banana

MY HOME: brushy shrub areas in North America

MY FOOD: seeds, fruits, and insects

MY SOUND: *purty-purty-purty*; also, *what-cheer, what-cheer*

Bright Blue Jays

BLUE JAYS HAVE CRESTS LIKE CARDINALS, BUT THE BIRDS **AREN'T RELATED.**

Blue jays love acorns from oak trees. They pluck them right off the tree branches. They hide the acorns under leaves on the ground to eat later. A blue jay can carry five acorns at a time!

CHECK ME OUT!

BLUE JAY

MY SIZE: about as long as a ruler

MY HOME: forests and parks in North America

MY FOOD: acorns, nuts, seeds, and small animals such as frogs and mice

MY SOUND: *jay, jay, jay*

Pretty Parrots

Parakeets are a kind of parrot. Nanday parakeets often live in groups of 10 or more birds, called colonies. These bright-green birds can be very noisy! They screech and squawk to talk to each other.

CHECK ME OUT! NANDAY PARAKEET

MY SIZE: about as long as a ruler

MY HOME: open fields in South America and parts of North America

MY FOOD: berries, seeds, and nuts

MY SOUND: kree-ah, kree-ah

MEET MORE PARROTS

HYACINTH MACAW

This bird is the largest of all parrots.

RED-AND-GREEN MACAW

These parrots often cling to the sides of clay cliffs in South America.

SULPHUR-CRESTED COCKATOO

These birds can imitate a dog's bark and other sounds.

SUN PARAKEET

The call of this small bird can be heard miles away.

Hopping Robins

Robins often hop on the ground looking for yummy snacks. Just like us, they eat different foods at different times. In the evening, robins nibble on fruits and berries. But for breakfast, they try to catch earthworms.

WHAT DO YOU LIKE TO EAT FOR BREAKFAST?

CHECK ME OUT! AMERICAN ROBIN

MY SIZE: about as long as an unsharpened pencil

MY HOME: lawns, fields, parks, woods, and forests in most of North America

MY FOOD: fruits, berries, earthworms, and snails

MY SOUND: *cheerily-cheer, up-cheerio*

Birds build their nests in places where their eggs will be safe. They use what they find nearby as building materials, such as twigs, mud, and even their own feathers.

AMERICAN ROBIN

American robins hide their nests under leafy branches.

CLIFF SWALLOW

Cliff swallows nest in colonies. They make nests from dried mud under bridges and roofs.

CLIFF SWALLOW EGGS ARE **COVERED IN BROWN SPECKLES.**

OSPREY

Ospreys make nests in high places, like on top of poles or dead trees.

CHIPPING SPARROW

Singing Sparrows

HOUSE SPARROW

Sparrows are songbirds. They whistle long tunes with lots of different sounds. Male song sparrows can sing more than 2,000 calls and songs in one day.

CHECK ME OUT! SONG SPARROW

MY SIZE: about as long as a dollar bill

MY HOME: brushy shrub areas in North America

MY FOOD: insects, seeds, and fruits

MY SOUND: *sweet-sweet-sweet;* also, *maids, maids, maids* and more

Different songs mean different things. For example, songs with fast cheeps tell other birds, "Stay away from my nest!"

WHAT SONGS DO YOU LIKE TO SING?

SONGBIRDS CAN **MAKE TWO DIFFERENT SOUNDS** AT THE SAME TIME.

BLACK-CAPPED CHICKADEE

Chickadees sound like they are calling their own name: *chickadee-dee-dee*.

Even More

PAINTED BUNTING

This bird's call sounds like a soft *plik*.

TUFTED TITMOUSE

The titmouse whistles *peter-peter-peter*.

SONGBIRDS

PURPLE FINCH

The song of this finch sounds like *hear-me?-see-me?-here-i-am.*

AMERICAN GOLDFINCH

This bright-yellow bird's call sounds like *po-ta-to-chip.*

EASTERN BLUEBIRD

This bird's call sounds like *tu-a-wee.*

Let's Talk Turkey!

Wild turkeys have bald heads and necks. Males have a flap of bumpy skin, called a wattle, hanging from their necks. It turns bright red when the bird is looking for a mate.

TURKEYS LOOK FLUFFY BECAUSE THEY HAVE **MORE THAN 5,000 FEATHERS.**

CHECK ME OUT! EASTERN WILD TURKEY

MY SIZE: about as tall as a baseball bat

MY HOME: fields and forests in North America

MY FOOD: seeds, nuts, acorns, and insects

MY SOUND: *gobble-gobble*

Speedy Quail

Quail are plump birds with short tails. They run on the ground more than they fly. The dark, curved feathers on its head make Gambel's quail easy to spot.

GAMBEL'S QUAIL CHICK

THESE CHICKS ARE **BORN READY TO RUN** AFTER THEIR PARENTS!

CHECK ME OUT! GAMBEL'S QUAIL

MY SIZE: about as big as a volleyball

MY HOME: deserts in southwest North America

MY FOOD: seeds, insects, berries, and cactus fruit

MY SOUND: chi-CA-go-go

Crafty Crows!

Crows are clever birds. Some crows use sticks as tools to dig up tasty worms deep in the ground. Crows are also noisy. They have many different calls. One call says that a cat is nearby. Another warns that a hawk has been spotted.

CHECK ME OUT! AMERICAN CROW

MY SIZE: about the length of a bowling pin

MY HOME: open areas with trees nearby across much of North America

MY FOOD: almost everything, including seeds, nuts, fruits, insects, and worms

MY SOUND: *caw-caw*

THERE ARE MORE THAN **30 KINDS OF CROWS** IN THE WORLD.

Perky Pigeons

Rock pigeons can be seen just about anywhere. Some live in barns on farms. Some make nests on window ledges. Rock pigeons are often found in city parks.

CHECK ME OUT!

ROCK PIGEON

MY SIZE: about the length of a ruler

MY HOME: cities and farms around the world, except Antarctica

MY FOOD: seeds, fruits, and earthworms

MY SOUND: *coo-cuk-cuk-cuk-cooo*

Watch Like a Hawk

Hawks often perch in tall trees. They watch the ground below. Hawks turn their heads a lot because they can't move their eyes. But hawks have super sight! When they spot a tiny mouse, they swoop down and grab it for dinner.

RED-TAILED HAWKS GET THEIR **RUSTY RED TAIL FEATHERS AS ADULTS.**

CHECK ME OUT! RED-TAILED HAWK

MY SIZE: about as long as a windshield wiper

MY HOME: mountains, prairies, deserts, and cities in North America

MY FOOD: mice, moles, reptiles, and birds

MY SOUND: *keee-eerrrrrr*

WHAT'S THE FARTHEST THING YOU CAN SEE?

Eagles Everywhere

There are about 60 kinds of eagles. They live all around the world, except Antarctica. Most eagles build large nests, and each year they add more sticks and grass to them. After many years, a bald eagle's nest can weigh as much as a small car!

CHECK ME OUT! BALD EAGLE

MY SIZE: about as tall as a dining room table

MY HOME: near lakes, rivers, and sometimes mountains in North America

MY FOOD: mainly fish, also small mammals, reptiles, and frogs

MY SOUND: *kwit kee-kee-kee-kee-keer*

A BALD EAGLE'S WINGSPAN CAN BE **LONGER THAN A BED.**

THIS BIRD'S **"HORNS"** ARE ACTUALLY MADE OF **SOFT FEATHERS.**

CHECK ME OUT! GREAT HORNED OWL

MY SIZE: about as tall as the arms of a sofa

MY HOME: forests throughout North, Central, and South America

MY FOOD: birds and small mammals such as rats and rabbits

MY SOUND: *hoo hoo-HOO hooo-hoo*

Outstanding Owls

Owls are birds of prey, like hawks and eagles. This means they hunt other animals. Most owls are nocturnal. They sleep during the day and hunt at night. Owls can rotate their heads almost all the way around to see what's behind them.

HOW FAR CAN YOU TURN YOUR HEAD?

MEET MORE OWLS

BARN OWL
This owl makes a *screeee-eech* sound.

SNOWY OWL
This white bird lives in cold places, where it blends in with the snow.

ELF OWL
The elf owl is the smallest owl. It is about the size of a juice box. It tucks its nest into a hole in a tree.

Just Ducky!

Not all ducks quack, but female mallards do. It's how they gather their ducklings together. When ducklings are about a day old, their mother leads them to the nearest water to look for food.

WEBBED FEET HELP DUCKS PADDLE IN THE WATER.

CHECK ME OUT! MALLARD

MY SIZE: about as long as two rulers end to end

MY HOME: ponds, lakes, and rivers in North America, Europe, and Asia

MY FOOD: seeds, stems, grasses, tiny fish, and other small animals

MY SOUND: *quack-quack-quack* (female); *rheab* (male)

DIVERS AND DABBLERS

Not all ducks find their food the same way.

GREEN-WINGED TEAL

Dabbling ducks, like the green-winged teal, just poke their heads underwater to find food.

HOW WOULD YOU CATCH A FISH?

HOODED MERGANSER

Diving ducks, like this hooded merganser, swim underwater to catch fish and insects.

NORTHERN PINTAIL

This duck has a long neck and long pointed tail feathers.

Meet More DUCKS

CANVASBACK

The canvasback is the largest of the diving ducks.

RUDDY DUCK

In the summer, a male ruddy duck's beak turns bright blue.

BUFFLEHEAD

The bufflehead is a small duck that makes its nest in old tree holes made by woodpeckers.

MUSCOVY DUCK

This duck has strong claws on its webbed feet that help it perch in tall trees.

GOOSE
ON THE LOOSE

Canada geese are related to ducks. They fly in a V formation. The geese take turns leading. As they fly, they call to each other: *honk-a-lonk!*

MALE DUCKS ARE CALLED **DRAKES.** MALE GEESE ARE CALLED **GANDERS.**

Go Fish, Heron!

The great blue heron is a wading bird. It stands in shallow water, waiting for a fish to swim by. Then—*snap!* It snatches the fish in its sharp beak and gulps it down.

THIS BIRD GROOMS ITS FEATHERS **WITH ITS MIDDLE TOE.**

CHECK ME OUT! GREAT BLUE HERON

MY SIZE: about as tall as a six-year-old child

MY HOME: near lakes, ponds, rivers, and marshes in North and South America

MY FOOD: fish, frogs, and snakes

MY SOUND: *roh-roh-roh; FRAWNK*

MEET MORE
WADING BIRDS

GLOSSY IBIS

Ibises use their curved beaks to pull food out of the mud.

AMERICAN FLAMINGO

Flamingos can sleep standing on one leg.

GREAT EGRET

These tall white birds have curvy necks.

WOOD STORK

Adult wood storks have bald heads.

CHECK ME OUT!

HERRING GULL

MY SIZE: about as tall as a bowling pin

MY HOME: near water in North America, Europe, and Asia

MY FOOD: shellfish, small fish, and worms

MY SOUND: *ha-ha-ha-ha kyow-kyow*

Clever Gulls

Herring gulls search the beach for buried clams. When a gull finds one, it digs up the clam and flies high in the sky with it. The gull drops the clamshell on a rock over and over again until it pops open. Dinner is ready!

MEET MORE BEACH BIRDS

ATLANTIC PUFFIN

A puffin can hold a lot of fish in its beak.

AMERICAN OYSTERCATCHER

This beach bird often makes its nest in the sand dunes.

BROWN PELICAN

This bird has a stretchy pouch attached to its bill that it fills with fish and water.

KAKAPO

They cannot fly, but these parrots can climb. Kakapos live in New Zealand.

OSTRICH

Ostriches live in Africa. They are the largest birds in the world.

Flightless BIRDS

SOUTHERN ROCKHOPPER PENGUIN

The rockhopper hops from rock to rock on islands near Antarctica.

SOUTHERN CASSOWARY

This big bird has a sharp claw on each foot. It lives in Australia.

NORTH ISLAND BROWN KIWI

These New Zealand birds have nostrils at the tip of their beaks.

KING PENGUIN

This penguin lives in the Antarctic region. It uses its wings to swim instead of fly!

Here are a few birds from around the world that walk, run, hop, or swim—but do not fly.

EMU

Emus can jump straight up into the air. They live in Australia.

CAN YOU SPEAK BIRD?

CAW **LIKE A CROW.**

SQUAWK **LIKE A PARAKEET.**

GOBBLE **LIKE A TURKEY.**

WHISTLE **LIKE A SPARROW.**

HOOT **LIKE AN OWL.**

QUACK **LIKE A DUCK.**

MOVE LIKE A BIRD!

PECK LIKE A **WOODPECKER.**

SPREAD YOUR ARMS WIDE LIKE WINGS, AND TRY OUT YOUR BEST **EAGLE** STARE!

FLAP YOUR ARMS FAST LIKE **HUMMINGBIRD** WINGS.

HOP ON TWO FEET LIKE A **ROBIN.**

LOOK AT THINGS BY MOVING ONLY YOUR HEAD LIKE A **HAWK.**

STAND ON ONE FOOT LIKE A **FLAMINGO.**

GLOSSARY

BALTIMORE ORIOLE

BACKBONE A set of connected bones down the middle of the back

BEAK The hard part of a bird's mouth, also called a bill

CALL A sound made by a bird that sends a message

COLONY A group of birds that live together

CREST A group of feathers on top of a bird's head

DOWN Fluffy feathers that baby birds have before their full feathers grow in

MALLARD

MAMMALS A group of animals, including humans, that have backbones, breathe air, have hair, and drink their mother's milk

MATE A partner in a pair of animals

MIGRATION The regular movement of birds or other animals from one place to another, usually when the season changes

NECTAR A sugary sweet liquid inside of flowers

NOCTURNAL Active during the night

ORNITHOLOGIST A scientist who studies birds

PERCH To sit or stand on the edge of something, like a branch

PREDATOR An animal that hunts other animals (prey) for food

PREY An animal that a predator hunts for food

REPTILE A group of animals, including lizards and snakes, that have backbones, scaly skin, and usually lay eggs

SAP The liquid that flows through a tree or other plant and carries water and food

SONG Pattern of notes, usually sung by a male bird

INDEX

Photo Credits

AS = Adobe Stock; SS = Shutterstock

Cover: (LO RT), Janet/AS; (LO LE), Chris Mattison/Nature Picture Library; (CTR LE), Svetlana Foote/SS; (UP LE), Chamnan Phanthong/AS; (UP RT), Madlen/SS; (RT), katpaws/AS; (CTR RT), Vera Kuttelvaserova/AS; Spine (CTR LE), Svetlana Foote/SS; Back cover: (UP LE), ondrejprosicky/AS; (UP RT), Jen/AS; (LO), Jennifer Davis/AS; 1, jimcumming88/AS; 2 (UP), Krzysztof Bubel/AS; 2 (LO), Susan Hodgson/SS; 3 (LO), Rick/AS; 3 (UP LE), Ivan/AS; 3 (UP CTR), kojihirano/AS; 3 (UP RT), kojihirano/AS; 4 (LO), Kent Weakley/SS; 4 (UP LE), olga demchishina/AS; 4 (UP RT), Sari ONeal/SS; 5 (LO RT), donyanedomam/AS; 5 (LO LE), Mettus/SS; 5 (CTR LE), Alan Murphy/Minden Pictures; 5 (UP LE), Pim Leijen/AS; 5 (UP CTR), David McGowen/AS; 5 (UP RT), Konstantin/AS; 6 (LE), ericlefrancais/SS; 6 (RT), Tatiana/AS; 6 (LO), Christopher Boswell/SS; 7 (UP LE), Wabb/AS; 7 (LO LE), WavebreakMediaMicro/AS; 7 (RT), BalanceFormCreative/AS; 8 (UP), katpaws/AS; 8 (UP), Vera Kuttelvaserova/AS; 8 (CTR LE), Menno Schaefer/SS; 8 (CTR CTR), FotoRequest/SS; 8 (CTR RT), Vladimir Seliverstov/Dreamstime; 8 (RT), Tony Moran/SS; 8 (LO LE), KarSol/SS; 8 (LO CTR), Ondrej Prosicky/SS; 9 (CTR), Mike Truchon/SS; 9 (LO RT), Krzysztof Bubel/AS; 9 (UP RT), jamie/AS; 10 (LO LE), mtruchon/AS; 10 (LO RT), Janet/AS; 10 (CTR LE), Alexey Stiop/AS; 10 (CTR RT), Reimar/AS; 10 (UP), kolesnikovserg/AS; 10 (UP), Le Do/AS; 11 (LO), Tom Reichner/SS; 11 (UP), Agnieszka Bacal/SS; 11 (CTR), haseg77/AS; 12, Nick Taurus/AS; 12 (UP), artesiawells/AS; 13 (UP), Steve Byland/AS; 13 (LO LE), Melinda Fawver/AS; 13 (LO CTR), BraulioLC/SS; 13 (LO RT), webguzs/Getty Images; 14-15, Kenneth Keifer/AS; 14 (UP), asharkyu/SS; 15 (UP), Hayley Crews/SS; 15 (CTR), Ed Schneider/SS; 15 (LO), Yakubovich Dmitry/AS; 16, Bonnie Taylor Barry/AS; 17 (RT), Mircea Costina/AS; 17 (UP LE), Dionisvera/AS; 17 (CTR LE), New Africa/AS; 17 (LO LE), Marie Read/Nature Picture Library; 18, Rodrigo S Coelho/AS; 18 (UP), Michael J. Cohen/Getty Images; 19 (UP LE), Ana Gram/AS; 19 (LO LE), Glenn Bartley/Minden Pictures; 19 (RT), dennisjacobsen/AS; 19 (LO CTR), Ken Griffiths/SS; 20, leekris/AS; 21 (LE), Greg Meland/AS; 21 (UP RT), Natalia Kuzmina/SS; 21 (LO CTR), elharo/AS; 21 (LO RT), photographybyJHWilliams/Getty Images; 22-23, GarysFRP/Getty Images; 22 (UP RT), raulbaena/AS; 22 (UP LE), AlekseyKarpenko/AS; 23 (RT), RLS Photo/AS; 24 (LE), Matthew Orselli/SS; 24 (UP RT), Steve Byland/AS; 24 (LO RT), rck/AS; 25 (UP LE), FotoRequest/AS; 25 (UP RT), Agnieszka Bacal/SS; 25 (LO), Bonnie Taylor Barry/AS; 26, Paul/AS; 27, Susan Hodgson/SS; 27 (UP RT), Charles/AS; 28, Chase D'Animulls/AS; 28 (UP), Valentina Razumova/SS; 29, Nuwat/AS; 29 (LO), stockphoto mania/SS; 30, ondrejprosicky/AS; 30 (LO), Eric Isselée/AS; 31, styxclick/AS; 31 (LO LE), harmantasdc/AS; 32-33, Dan Sullivan/Alamy Stock Photo; 32 (UP LE), donyanedomam/AS; 33 (LO LE), Monikasurzin/AS; 33 (LO CTR), rtaylorimages/AS; 33 (LO RT), hstiver/Getty Images; 34, Helen Davies/AS; 34 (UP RT), Dagny Louise Rekaa/SS; 35 (LE), Susan Hodgson/AS; 35 (LO RT), David/AS; 35 (UP RT), Anthony Bower/AS; 36 (UP LE), tomreichner/AS; 36-37 (UP), tomreichner/AS; 36-37 (LO), Brian E Kushner/AS; 37 (CTR RT), Richard/AS; 37 (LE), Chase D'animulls/SS; 37 (LO RT), Colin Temple/AS; 37 (UP RT), Russell/AS; 38, William/AS; 39 (UP LE), kajornyot/AS; 39 (LO LE), Abeselom Zerit/AS; 39 (LO CTR), FloridaStock/SS; 39 (RT), naturelight/AS; 40-41, Alan Tunnicliffe Photography/Getty Images; 41 (LO LE), creativenature.nl/AS; 41 (LO CTR), Brian E Kushner/AS; 41 (LO RT), Yarkovoy/AS; 41 (UP LE), filin174/AS; 41 (UP RT), uckyo/AS; 42 (UP LE), Stephen Belcher/Minden Pictures; 42-43 (UP), art_zzz/AS; 42-43 (LO), Danny Ye/SS; 42 (LO LE), Jaynes Gallery/Danita Delimont/AS; 43 (UP LE), miropa20/AS; 43 (LO LE), Ken Griffiths/SS; 43 (RT), herraez/AS; 44 (UP RT), tomreichner/AS; 44 (UP LE), pierre leclerc/EyeEm/AS; 44 (UP CTR), bijoustarr/AS; 44 (LO LE), Yuval Helfman/AS; 44 (LO CTR), Lori Ellis/AS; 44 (LO RT), merrimonc/AS; 45 (UP RT), Eric M. Berlin/AS; 45 (UP CTR), FloridaStock/AS; 45 (LO LE), Sean Xu/SS; 45 (LO CTR), Guan Jiangchi/AS; 45 (LO RT), gjohnstonphoto/Getty Images; 45 (UP LE), Iizuna Design/SS; 46 (UP), Mike Truchon/SS; 46 (LO), Aksenova Natalya/SS; 46 (LO RT), Vera Kuttelvaserova/AS; 46 (LO CTR), katpaws/AS

To my agent, Jennifer Unter, who gives my work wings —M.R.D.

Front cover birds (clockwise from top): red-and-green macaw, northern cardinal, blue jay; back cover birds (clockwise from top left): fiery-throated hummingbird, American robin; title page bird: snowy owl.

Published by National Geographic Partners, LLC, Washington, DC 20036

Designed by Sanjida Rashid

The publisher gratefully acknowledges National Geographic bird expert Jonathan Alderfer for his expert review of this book, and Dr. Tovah P. Klein, director of the Barnard College Center for Toddler Development, for her advice and expertise. Many thanks also to researcher Alicia Klepeis, photo editor Colin Wheeler, project editor Emily Fego, production editor Molly Reid, and associate designers Lauren Sciortino and David Marvin.

Library of Congress Cataloging-in-Publication Data
Names: Donohue, Moira Rose, author.
Title: Birds / Moira Rose Donohue.
Other titles: Birds
Description: Washington, DC : National Geographic Kids, [2024] | Series: Little kids first nature guide | Includes index. | Audience: Ages 4-8 | Audience: Grades K-1
Identifiers: LCCN 2022059103 | ISBN 9781426375392 (paperback) | ISBN 9781426375460 (library binding)
Subjects: LCSH: Birds--Juvenile literature.
Classification: LCC QL676.2 .D66 2024 | DDC 598--dc23/eng/20230206
LC record available at https://lccn.loc.gov/2022059103

Printed in China
23/RRDH/1